INFORMATION
EXPLORER
JUNIOR

Starting Your Own Blog

by Kristin Fontichiaro

CHERRY LAKE PUBLISHING · ANN ARBOR, MICHIGAN

CHERRY LAKE
Publishing

A NOTE TO PARENTS AND TEACHERS: Please remind your children how to stay safe online before they do the activities in this book.

A NOTE TO KIDS: Always remember your safety comes first!

Published in the United States of America
by Cherry Lake Publishing
Ann Arbor, Michigan
www.cherrylakepublishing.com

Content Adviser: Gail Dickinson, PhD, Associate Professor, Old Dominion University, Norfolk, Virginia

Photo Credits: Cover, ©karelnoppe/Shutterstock, Inc.; page 5, ©AlexKalashnikov/Shutterstock, Inc.; page 6, ©Andreas Gradin/Shutterstock, Inc.; page 11, ©wavebreakmedia/Shutterstock, Inc.; page 14, ©Michelle Milliman/Dreamstime.com; page 19, ©Jose Wilson Araujo/Dreamstime.com.

Library of Congress Cataloging-in-Publication Data
Fontichiaro, Kristin.
  Starting your own blog / by Kristin Fontichiaro.
    pages cm. — (Information explorer junior)
  Audience: Grades K to 3.
  Includes bibliographical references and index.
  ISBN 978-1-62431-133-8 (lib. bdg.) — ISBN 978-1-62431-199-4 (e-book) — ISBN 978-1-62431-265-6 (pbk.)
1. Blogs—Juvenile literature. I. Title.

  TK5105.8884.F663 2013
  006.7'52—dc23   2013005607

Cherry Lake Publishing would like to acknowledge the work of The Partnership for 21st Century Skills. Please visit www.p21.org for more information.

Printed in the United States of America
Corporate Graphics Inc.
July 2013
CLFA13

Table of Contents

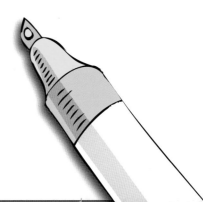

CHAPTER ONE

What Is a Blog?

Wow! Your class just got a new baby hamster! It is tiny, and it has hardly any fur. How can you keep track of how it is growing and what it is doing? Maybe you could start a **blog**!

Keeping a blog is like writing in a journal on the Web. In a paper journal, your writing is private and you might keep it locked away. But on the Web, other people can see your writing. You can use words, sound, video, and photos to share your thinking with others. Whenever you have something to share, you create a new **post** that shows up at the top of your Web page.

A blog post about the baby hamster might include the following:

Visitors to your blog might love to watch your hamster exercise on its wheel.

- **text** where you describe what the hamster eats every day
- photos showing how the hamster changes as it grows
- a video of the hamster running on a wheel
- a recording of the noise the hamster makes
- all of the above!

A blog about your soccer team could help your friends and relatives see how your season is going.

Blogs are a great way to let people know what you are doing, thinking, and planning right as it is happening. You can write a blog by yourself or be part of a blogging group. What interesting things are happening on your sports team? In class? At your after-school club? What books or TV shows could you talk about? All of these can be discussed on a blog. It's fun to look back and read what you wrote a month or a year ago!

To get a copy of this activity, visit www.cherrylakepublishing.com/activities.

Try This

With a friend, make a list of subjects you could blog about. Think about the things you do in your classroom, school, church group, sports team, hobby group, or community. What would be fun to write about and share with others?

CHAPTER TWO

Parts of a Blog

Blogs are Web pages filled with many kinds of information. They can have many designs and **layouts**, but all blogs share some of the same features.

The **URL** is the Web address that a visitor can type to visit your blog. You can find the URL at the top of your screen when you have a Web browser open.

You will find the blog header below the URL. The header usually includes a wide image to decorate the blog. It also shows the blog title, which is the name you give to your blog, such as *Our Hamster Is Growing*. The header and title will show up at the top of each page of your blog. Some blogs also let

Our Hamster Is Growing
A Class Blog

The header usually shows the title of a blog.

you give your blog a subtitle. A subtitle gives more information. For a blog with the title *Our Hamster Is Growing*, the subtitle could be *A Class Blog* or *Room 102*. You can also leave the subtitle blank.

Most of your screen will show the **body** of the blog. This is the area where blog posts are shown. Posts are made up of text, words, photos, video, or sound files. Each post gets its own title. It also has the date the blog post was written and the name of the author. Underneath the blog post, readers can write short messages back to the author. These messages are called **comments**.

Some blogs also have sidebars. These are tall, thin panels on the side of the screen that have extra information. You might find links to other Web sites or older blog posts there.

When you choose a **template** for your blog, have fun picking out a design and a layout that you like and that matches what you are writing about. You can change it whenever you want!

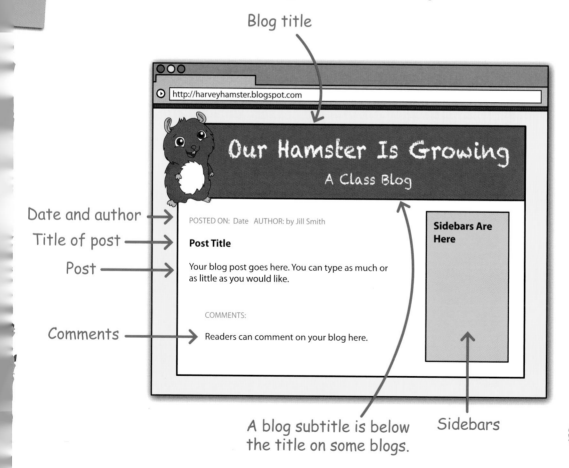

Blog title

http://harveyhamster.blogspot.com

Our Hamster Is Growing
A Class Blog

Date and author → POSTED ON: Date AUTHOR: by Jill Smith

Title of post → **Post Title**

Post → Your blog post goes here. You can type as much or as little as you would like.

COMMENTS:

Comments → Readers can comment on your blog here.

Sidebars Are Here

Sidebars

A blog subtitle is below the title on some blogs.

10

CHAPTER THREE

Name Your Blog

Ask an adult to help you set up your blog.

You can ask your parents to help you set up a blog using a site like *www.blogger.com* or *www.wordpress.com*. At school, your teacher might also use a Web site such as *www.kidblog.org* to set up a private blog for each student in the class. You, your teacher, and your classmates can see it, but other people cannot. This is a great way to start blogging safely.

Next, choose a title for your blog. Pick a title that tells people something about you or your topic. Here are some titles for a hamster blog:

- Harry the Hamster
- Room 102 Got a Hamster!
- Watch Our Hamster Grow!
- Our Hamster

Once you have a title, you can pick a URL for your blog. If you are using Blogger, you need to think of something that will fit in this blank: http://_____.blogspot.com. For WordPress, you need to fill in the blank here: http://_____.wordpress.com. If you are using Kidblog, your teacher will tell you your URL.

Pick your URL carefully. Every blog must have a different URL, so brainstorm backup choices in case someone is already using the URL you want. Use lowercase letters only. When you are choosing your blog title or URL, don't give away personal information such as your last name or address.

Let's look at the earlier title examples and give them some sample URLs:

- http://harveyhamster.blogspot.com
- http://room102hamster.wordpress.com
- http://growinghamster.blogspot.com

http://harveyhamster.blogspot.com

Be sure to choose a good URL for your blog!

Once your blog has been created and
named, it's time to pick out a design. Every
blogging site offers many templates or
themes you can choose from to change the
look of your blog. Find one with colors, a
layout, and pictures that match what you
are writing about.

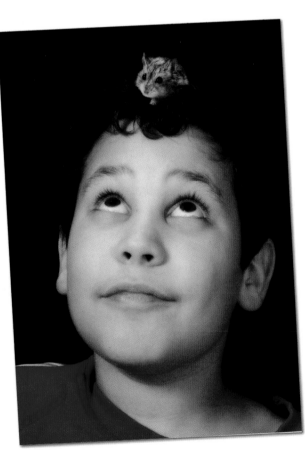

What colors and
pictures would
look good on a blog
about hamsters?

To get a copy of this activity, visit www.cherrylakepublishing.com/activities.

Try This

Look at the list of topics you brainstormed in chapter 1. Brainstorm possible blog titles and URLs to go with the different topics. Next, think about the colors and images that might match.

Choose one of these ideas. Then work with an adult to set up your blog. Pick a title, URL, and theme.

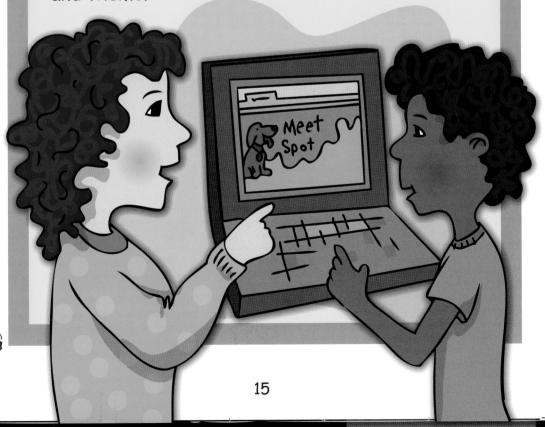

CHAPTER FOUR

Writing Your First Blog Post

Your blog is set up and ready to go. Are you ready to write?

Every blog post has two parts: a title and a body. The title is a lot like a newspaper headline. It should tell what your post is about. The body is the main part of the post. It contains your words, photos, videos, and more.

In your first blog post, say hello and explain why you are starting a blog. If you want, you can add photos, audio, or video, too. Read the blog site's directions to find out how.

For a hamster blog, your first post might look like this:

http://harveyhamster.blogspot.com

Our Hamster Is Growing
A Class Blog

POSTED ON: September 15, 2013, by Jill Smith

Hi! Welcome to Our Hamster Blog!

Welcome to Room 102's blog. We got a surprise today.
Mrs. J brought us a baby hamster! Its eyes are closed.
It does not look furry.

Your first post should explain
what your blog is about.

To get a copy of this activity, visit www.cherrylakepublishing.com/activities.

Try This

Time to start writing! Pick one of the topics you brainstormed earlier, and write a blog post.

But before you do, which of the following would be OK to mention online? What information should you keep offline? Talk about these with an adult:

- your first name
- your pet's name
- your favorite
  TV shows
- your school
- your teacher's name
- your phone number
- your address
- your e-mail address

SPOT

CHAPTER FIVE

Blog Comments

Sharing interesting blogs with family is fun.

Blogs are fun to write. They are also fun to read! When you read a blog post that you really like, you can tell the author how much you enjoyed it. Most blogs let readers write comments at the bottom of the posts. This can turn a blog into a conversation between an author and a reader.

When you write a comment, be sure to

- *Be polite*. Don't hurt the author's feelings. Be kind instead.

- *Be helpful*. Sometimes an author will ask for your help or a teacher will ask you to give feedback. For example, a blog author might ask readers to suggest ways to improve the blog. "Make better posts!" does not give the author any ideas for how to make it better. "I loved the photo of the baby hamster when it was sleeping. But I would like to see a picture of the hamster when it is awake!" gives the author a helpful suggestion.

- *Be specific*. A comment like "Great post" is nice. But it doesn't tell the writer anything about why you liked it. Here's a more specific comment: "It was funny when you told the story about the hamster eating toilet paper tubes." This lets the writer know exactly what he or she did well.

To get a copy of this activity, visit www.cherrylakepublishing.com/activities.

Try This

Which of the following comments would be good to leave on someone's blog? Which would you like to receive on your blog?

- The video of the hamster running on the wheel was so funny. Please post more videos!
- The close-up photo looks great!
- This is awful.
- Good job!
- I don't get it.
- Thanks.

Be polite, helpful, and specific when you write a comment.

Now you know how to set up, write, and read blogs. Have fun writing and sharing your ideas with your classmates, friends, and family!

Glossary

blog (BLAWG) a Web site that is like an online journal, where you can easily add new information

body (BAH-dee) the main area of a blog post, where you include text, audio, photos, or video

comments (KAH-ments) a reader's written responses to a blog post

layouts (LAY-outs) ways of organizing information, images, and other elements on a Web page

post (POHST) an individual entry in a blog

template (TEM-pluht) a premade layout for a blog that includes the frame of colors, images, and designs that surround blog posts

text (TEKST) words

themes (THEEMZ) designs for a Web page

URL (YOO AR EL) stands for Uniform Resource Locator, another way of saying Web address

Find Out More

BOOKS

Cornwall, Phyllis. *Mind Your Manners Online*. Ann Arbor, MI: Cherry Lake, 2012.

Mack, James. *Journals and Blogging*. Chicago: Raintree, 2009.

Raatma, Lucia. *Blogs*. Ann Arbor, MI: Cherry Lake, 2010.

WEB SITES

The Edublog Awards
http://edublogawards.com/2012awards/best-student-blogs-of-2012
Find award-winning blogs in the Best Student Blog category and get inspired!

Kidblog
http://kidblog.org
This site allows teachers to set up free, safe blogs for kids in their classroom.

Mrs. Yollis' Classroom Blog
http://yollisclassblog.blogspot.com
Visit Mrs. Yollis's third-grade class online. This blog won the Edublog Award for Best Class Blog in 2011. You can see the class blog and links to students' individual blogs.

Index

About the Author

Kristin Fontichiaro teaches at the University of Michigan School of Information. She reads blogs every morning and has been writing blog posts for years.